Introduction

The Steamship collection at the Science Museum includes a wide range of models, drawings and paintings showing the development of passenger vessels, warships, cargo ships and ancillary craft. Larger scale models of sections of ships, framing, bow and stern members, plating and welded construction illustrate the principal alterations and improvements in ship construction.

The collection is one of the oldest in the museum: indeed the Marine Construction collection, formed in 1864 when the Royal School of Naval Architecture was established at South Kensington, was the first engineering collection at the institution then known as the South Kensington Museum and, since 1909, as the Science Museum.

In this booklet it is only possible to give a very brief summary of the development of the steamship. Nineteen models, described and illustrated in chronological order, have been selected to show something of the early experimental steamboats and the various types of paddle and screw steamships launched before 1880. This termination at 1880 is arbitrary; merchant steamers launched after 1880 and motorships will be dealt with in a subsequent booklet.

In the simplest sense the mechanically propelled vessel originated when man first applied muscular force to paddles or oars to move his craft through the water. No definite date can be given for the introduction of the paddle-wheel for the propulsion of a vessel, but a bas-relief of 527 AD shows what is believed to be a Roman war vessel fitted with six small paddle-wheels and driven by three pairs of oxen. Warships with two paddle-wheels on each side, presumably driven by man-power, are said to have been used in China in the 8th century AD and in Europe manuscripts from the 15th century show designs for boats driven by paddle-wheels turned by men or animals. A Frenchman, Denis Papin, proposed in 1690 but never built a vessel with paddle-wheels to be driven by steam.

In 1736 Jonathan Hulls of Gloucestershire patented a design for a boat in which a stern paddle-wheel was to have been driven by a Newcomen 'atmospheric' engine. The steam engines of that time were, however, too heavy in relation to their power for practical trials to be made. (The introduction of marine steam propulsion depended closely on the previous development of the land engine and detailed information about this development can be found in the Science Museum booklet *The Steam Engine* by R.J. Law.)

The first boat actually to be driven by steam power was that used by J. C. Perier, on the river Seine near Paris in 1775, and during the last quarter of the 18th century, a number of experimental steam boats were built. In France experiments in steam propulsion were carried out by the Marquis de Jouffroy d'Abbans and in 1783 his vessel the *Pyroscaphe* was propelled for 15 minutes against the current of the river Saone, near Lyons, by paddle-wheels driven by a steam engine. In America, James Rumsey of Virginia and John Fitch of Pennsylvania were engaged in pioneer work on marine steam propulsion. In 1785 Rumsey employed hydraulic jet propulsion for a boat. A steam-driven pump was used to draw water in at the bow of the vessel and force it out at the stern. John Fitch experimented with several types of paddle-wheels and in 1790 he initiated a service on the river Delaware, with a boat which had a beam type of engine, with a cylinder 18 in diameter, driving three 'duck-leg' paddle-boards at the stern.

In Scotland, Patrick Miller developed a double-hulled vessel propelled by paddle-wheels driven by capstans worked by manual

A Science Museum
illustrated booklet

STEAMSHIPS

1: Merchant ships to 1880

by B. W. Bathe

Her Majesty's Stationery
Office London 1969

SBN 11 290025 9

Cover: P.S. 'Britannia', 1840 (see plate 10)

Note: All the items illustrated in this booklet are part of the Science Museum collections

power. In 1788 Miller fitted a steam engine, specially designed by William Symington, to one hull of a double-hulled vessel and the boiler on the other hull. The engine was connected by gearing to two paddle-wheels situated, one in front of the other, in the space between the two hulls. On trials the vessel is said to have attained a speed of 5 miles per hour.

In the early years of the 19th century more and more attention was given to steam power as a serious competitor to sail and its potential advantages for trade and passenger traffic were being realised.

The *Charlotte Dundas* (Plate 1) built in Scotland in 1801 has been described as 'the first practical steamboat'. The *Charlotte Dundas* was used on the Forth and Clyde canal for experiments on the use of steam tugs instead of horses for towing vessels.

The experimental steamboat (Plate 2) built in Paris in 1803 for the American Robert Fulton, broke in half during a storm and sank while moored in the river Seine before the vessel could be tested. The machinery was retrieved, however, and fitted to a new hull of somewhat heavier construction. After successful trials with this steamboat Fulton returned to America and ordered the paddle-boat *Clermont* to be built in New York. On August 17th, 1807 the *Clermont* attained a speed of 4·7 miles per hour on the river Hudson between Albany and New York, The vessel was used as a packet on this route in 1807 and after being rebuilt and refitted continued in use on the Hudson for many years.

The *Comet* (Plate 3), launched in 1812, was employed as a public conveyance for passengers on the river Clyde between Glasgow and Helensburgh and was the first paddle steamer to run commercially in Europe.

Steam propulsion was soon firmly established as an alternative to sail for river and coastwise traffic but not for ocean-going ships, which retained a very considerable spread of sail. Engines were unreliable and had to be stopped frequently so that accumulated salt could be cleared from the boilers, an operation which entailed heavy coal consumption; and coaling stations were far apart. But the introduction in the 1830's of a practical surface condenser which could supply the boilers with fresh water brought about a substantial saving in the coal used on a long voyage. The first steam-propelled vessel to cross the Atlantic, or in fact any ocean, was the American ship *Savannah* (Plate 4), a fully rigged vessel fitted with an engine and detachable paddle-wheels which could be stowed on deck when not in use. The *Savannah* sailed from New York on the 24th May, 1818, and arrived off the coast of Ireland on the 17th June. The greater part of the crossing was made under sail alone.

The small steamships of the 1830's were considered suitable for long voyages. The PS *William Fawcett* (Plate 6), although intended for service as a ferry-boat on the river Mersey, was purchased in 1837 by the Peninsular Steam Navigation Co in order to start their contract mail service to Gibraltar. In the same year another little cross-channel steamer, the PS *Sirius* (Plate 8), was the first vessel to cross the Atlantic under continuous steam power. Her engines were of the side-lever type, a development from the original simple beam engine which was unsuitable owing to its high centre of gravity. The side-lever type of engine became the most popular for paddle-steamers, but it was cumbersome and the oscillating engine, giving greater power for less space and weight, came into use. Finally, in the 1860's, came high pressure steam and the compound-expansion engine.

The PS *Great Western* (Plate 9) was the first steamship designed and constructed specially for the service across the Atlantic. Her first crossing of the ocean was accomplished in April 1838 at a mean speed of 8·8 knots and fully demonstrated the practicability of ocean steamship transport. Two years later the first regular monthly transatlantic steamship service was established with the

PS *Britannia* (Plate 10) and her sister ships the *Acadia, Caledonia* and *Columbia*.

Although iron barges had been built and used in the 1780's, many experienced shipbuilders opposed the construction of iron-hulled vessels. However, the advantages of building in iron instead of wood were accepted gradually and the first iron steamship the PS *Aaron Manby* was built in 1821. In 1838 Lloyd's Register of Shipping admitted iron ships to A1 classification and in the early 1850's more than 150 iron ships were registered, about two-thirds being steamships.

With iron construction and more efficient engines, steamships increased in size and the disadvantages of the paddle-wheel became more apparent. Experiments had been made with screw propulsion since the early days of steam and by the 1840's the propeller was beginning to take the place of the paddle-wheel. The SS *Great Britain* (Plate 11) was the first iron-built screw-propelled vessel to cross the Atlantic under steam.

The PSS *Great Eastern* (Plates 14 and 15) has been described, perhaps somewhat unfairly, as 'the greatest failure in the whole history of marine engineering; a premature leviathan conceived and built forty years in advance of practical experience'. This great vessel measured 18,914 tons gross, with a length of 680 ft and was unique in that she was propelled both by paddle-wheels and a screw propeller.

The finest paddle-steamer constructed for the Atlantic service, the *Scotia* (Plate 17) launched in 1861, attained a speed of 16·5 knots on trial and her fastest crossing of the Atlantic was made in 8 days 3 hours. However, the era of the Atlantic paddle-steamer was nearly over and the record crossing made in 1867 by the screw-propelled Atlantic liner *City of Paris* (Plate 19) probably influenced the decision to abandon paddle-steamers for the Atlantic service.

1 P.T. 'Charlotte Dundas', 1801

This famous early steamboat, commissioned by Lord Dundas of Kerse and named after his daughter, was designed as a tug for experiments on the Forth and Clyde Canal.

The *Charlotte Dundas*, 56 ft in length with a beam of 18 ft, was built of wood by Alexander Hart at Grangemouth Dockyard. The engine, made by William Symington with a single horizontal double-acting cylinder 22 in diameter and 4 ft stroke, was placed on the port side of the deck. The piston rod was guided in slides, and the connecting-rod acted directly on an overhung crank on the paddle-wheel shaft, an arrangement patented by Symington in 1801. The jet condenser and vertical air pump were below deck, the pump being worked by a bell-crank from the crosshead. Steam was supplied by a boiler arranged on the starboard side of the boat. The engine drove a single paddle-wheel placed at the stern of the vessel.

In March 1802, two loaded vessels, each of 70 tons burden, were successfully towed by the *Charlotte Dundas* on the canal for a distance of 19·5 miles in six hours against a strong adverse wind. This performance was satisfactory, but the canal owners decided that any benefit resulting from the use of steam tugs would not compensate for the damage that would be done to the canal banks by the wash of the paddles, and the proposal to use steam tugs was therefore rejected. The *Charlotte Dundas* was laid up for many years in a creek of the canal, and in 1861 she was finally broken up.

2 Fulton's first steamboat, 1803

The American pioneer of marine steam propulsion, Robert Fulton, had an experimental steamboat built in Paris in 1803. After the boat had been completed and was moored in the river Seine ready for steam trials, a violent storm arose. The wooden hull, 66·5 ft in length, proved unequal to the weight of the machinery in such circumstances; it broke in half and the whole sank into the mud of the river. However the machinery was recovered and fitted to a hull of somewhat heavier construction. On trial this boat towed two vessels for $1\frac{1}{2}$ hours at a speed of about 4 miles per hour.
The engine, with a vertical upright double-acting cylinder, was rated at 8 nominal horse power. The crosshead at the upper end of the piston rod worked in vertical guides from which the motion was taken down by return connecting-rods to a pair of bell-crank side-levers. From the upper point of these, the drive was taken by a horizontal connecting rod, to the paddle crankshaft. The paddle-wheels were 12 ft diameter, each with ten fixed radial float boards.

Note: In the first half of the 19th century, the 'Nominal horse power' of a steam engine given by the formula $\frac{d^2 \times \sqrt[3]{S}}{47}$ (where 'S' = length of stroke in feet and 'd' = diameter of cylinder in inches) was used as a comparative measure of the power of a marine engine. From the mid 19th century, with higher piston speeds and boiler pressures, 'Indicated horse power' a measure of the actual power developed in the cylinders was also used to show the very much greater power actually available.

3 P.S. 'Comet', 1812

Encouraged, perhaps, by reports of the success of steamboats in America, Henry Bell had a vessel built at Glasgow in 1811-12 for a passenger service on the Clyde. The paddle-steamer was named after the famous comet of 1811 and achieved a place in history as the first steamer to run commercially in Europe.

The *Comet*, built of wood, was 51 ft long with a breadth over the paddle boxes of 15 ft. The engine, of 4 nominal hp, with a single upright cylinder 12 in diameter by 16 in stroke was placed on the port side of the vessel and the boiler, set in brickwork, on the starboard. At first there were two sets of radial paddles on each side, driven by spur gear, but as this arrangement gave trouble, paddle-wheels were afterwards substituted, and the number of wheels was reduced to two; the steaming speed was about 6·7 knots. There was a single funnel, which served also as a mast and carried a yard and square sail.

In August 1812 the vessel commenced running on the Clyde between Glasgow and Greenock, as a public conveyance for passengers at the advertised fares of 4s for the first cabin and 3s for the second.

In 1816 the *Comet* was used on the Firth of Forth, and in 1818 Bell employed her in establishing steam communication between the West Highlands and Glasgow; in 1820 she went ashore at Graignish Point and became a total wreck.

COMET.

4 P.S. 'Savannah', 1818

In 1818, while river and coastal steamboats were being used to establish regular services in many parts of the world, ocean-going sailing ships were just beginning to have auxiliary engines fitted to assist the power of sail.

This was the case with the *Savannah*, a small wood sailing ship of 320 tons with a length of 110 ft. Built in New York in 1818 for the sail-packet service to France, she was bought before completion by the Savannah Steamship Company and fitted with an auxiliary engine.

The engine, of 58 nominal hp, had one cylinder 40in diameter by 5 ft stroke. Steam was supplied by copper boilers with riveted flues. The pressure is said to have been less than 1 lb per sq in above atmospheric. The smoke pipe was fitted at the top with an elbow, which could be turned as necessary, to direct the smoke and sparks away from the sails.

The paddle-wheels were 15·25 ft diameter, and were made collapsible. Each had ten radial arms which could be folded up like a fan and taken on deck when not in use.

In 1819 the *Savannah* made the journey from Savannah to Liverpool in 27 days 11 hours and thus became the first 'steamship' to cross an ocean, although her engine was only used for about 85 hours in all. Her speed under steam alone was about 6 knots. Steam power was still so new that when she was seen off the coast of Ireland she was reported as a ship on fire. The *Savannah* later went to Russia, from whence she returned to New York under sail. Her engine was then removed and she was used for a short time as a coastal sail-packet before being wrecked in 1821.

5 P.S. 'City of Bristol', 1827

Launched at Bristol in 1827, the *City of Bristol* was 143·8 ft long with a breadth over the paddle boxes of 35·2 ft. The vessel was used on the service between Bristol and Dublin, run by the War Office Steam Packet Co, which held contracts to transport troops, recruits and convicts to and from Ireland.

The *City of Bristol* was rigged as a two-masted schooner, and her engines of 160 nominal hp were doubtless of the side-lever type introduced by Messrs Boulton, Watt and Co, with two cylinders about 48 in diameter by 60 in stroke. The boiler pressure would have been about 3 lb per sq in. The paddle-wheels were 12 ft diameter, each with 12 fixed radial floats 6 ft long and 13 in wide, and rotated at 30 revs per min. The speed of the vessel would be about 8 knots in favourable weather.

The *City of Bristol* ran her trials in March 1828. It is stated in contemporary records that the 'expectations of the proprietors as to her capacity of speed and the working of her machinery were fully realised, while the comfort and elegance of her interior arrangements excited the admiration of the company.' The vessel was wrecked at Worms Head in November 1840, while homeward bound from Waterford.

6 P.S. 'William Fawcett', 1829

This small paddle-steamer was built of wood in 1829 by Caleb Smith of Liverpool, for use as a ferry-boat on the river Mersey. She was later placed on the Belfast, Dublin and London service of the Dublin and London Steam Packet Co, from whom she was purchased in 1837 by the newly formed Peninsular Steam Navigation Co, in order to start their contract mail service between Falmouth and Gibraltar, with calls at intermediate ports on the Atlantic seaboard of Spain and Portugal.

The *William Fawcett* was only 87 ft long and had accommodation for 12 passengers in cabins and saloon under her raised quarter deck. She had a short forecastle above her clipper bow, carried three lifeboats, and was decorated with mock quarter-galleries at the stern. Three square sails were carried on the foremast and a loose-footed gaff on the mainmast.

In addition to her considerable spread of sail, the vessel was propelled by a pair of side-lever engines of 60 nominal hp, constructed by Fawcett, Preston and Co of Liverpool. The diameter of the cylinders was 43·5 in, the stroke 4 ft 6 in. The paddle-wheels were 15 ft 3 in diameter; each with 12 fixed radial floats 4 ft 3 in wide. The speed of the vessel was 8 knots in favourable weather.

7 P.T. 'Monarch', 1833

The use of a steam engine for propelling a vessel gave it independence of wind and tide; a factor of particular importance for tug-boats. This was realised by Jonathan Hulls as early as 1736 when he was granted a patent for a steam driven towing-boat more than fifty years before such a proposal could become a working reality.

The first steam-propelled vessels in the British Navy were used to tow the sailing warships in and out of harbour.

The *Monarch* was built of wood in 1833 for service on the river Thames and was the first steam tug owned by Messrs William Watkins, Ltd of London.

Her single-cylinder engine of 20 nominal hp was supplied with steam by a flue boiler, which in 1845 was replaced by a tubular boiler. The bunkers stowed 7 tons of coal. The paddle-wheels were about 8 ft 9 in diameter and 3 ft wide, but were not disconnectable. In order to improve the manoeuvrability of the vessel means were provided for inclining her, so as to lift one paddle-wheel either wholly or partially out of the water. The arrangement consisted of an iron tank filled with fire-bars and iron chain and mounted on rails, which could be pushed to either side of the deck. The *Monarch* was fitted with new paddle-wheels in 1856, and another new boiler in 1861. She was sold for scrap in 1876.

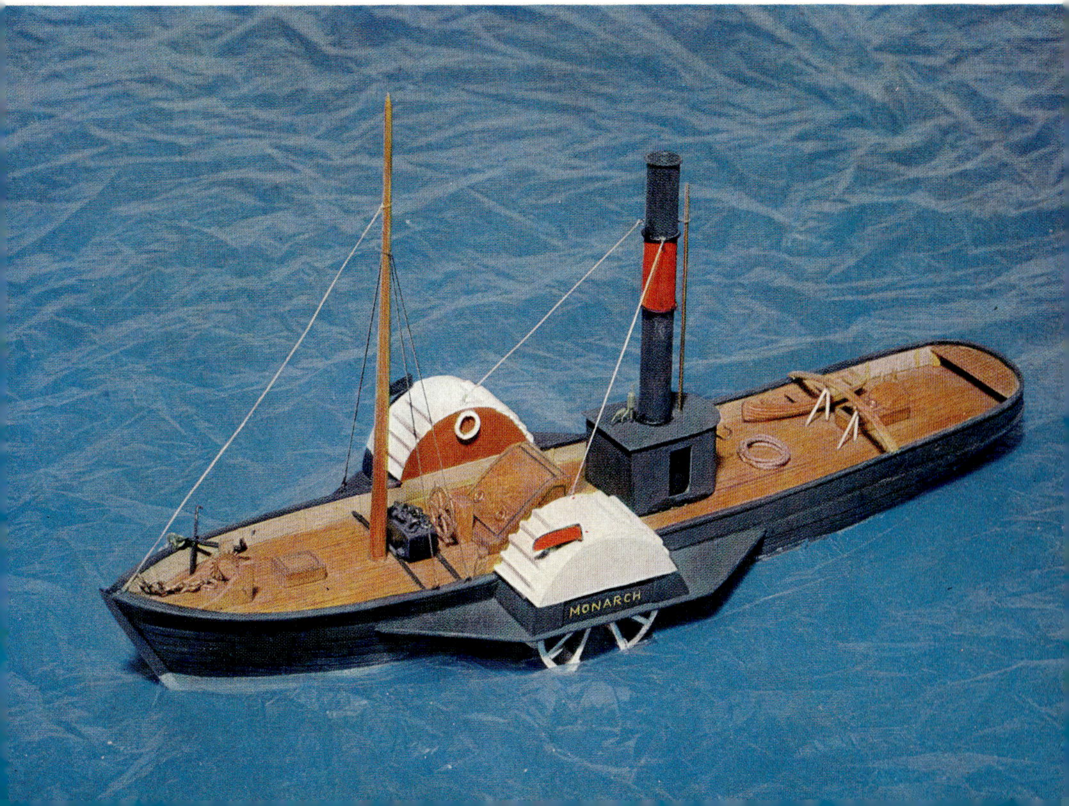
MONARCH

8 P.S. 'Sirius', 1837

Although never intended for the Atlantic service, this little cross-channel steamer, only 208 ft in length and 703 tons gross, was the first vessel to cross the Atlantic under continuous steam power.

The *Sirius* was built of wood at Leith in 1837 for the service between London and Cork. Her engines of 320 nominal hp were of the side-lever type with two cylinders each having a diameter of 60 in with a stroke of 6 ft. A notable feature of the machinery was the use of a surface condenser, patented by Samuel Hall in 1834, which enabled her boilers to be fed with fresh water. Steam at a pressure of 5 lb per sq in was supplied by rectangular flue boilers, which consumed about 24 tons of coal per day. The paddle-wheels had a diameter of 24 ft and made 15 revolutions per minute for a speed of about 9 knots.

The *Sirius* was chartered by the British and American Steam Navigation Co and left Cork Harbour, with 40 passengers, on the 4th April 1838, reaching New York in 18 days 10 hours at a mean speed of 6·7 knots. Her arrival at New York occasioned great enthusiasm and she was sent off on her return voyage by a crowd of thousands and a salute of seventeen guns. After a second double crossing the *Sirius* returned to the short sea crossing service for which she had been intended, until wrecked in 1847.

9 P.S. 'Great Western', 1837

This was the first steamer constructed specially for the Atlantic Ferry service.

The *Great Western* was built of wood at Bristol to the plans of I.K. Brunel and launched in July 1837 for the Great Western Steamship Co. The hull, 236 ft long, was constructed with very heavy frames and internal bracing of iron and wood diagonal trusses and shelf-pieces, giving great longitudinal strength. The saloon, 75 ft long, is said to have been the largest and most luxurious room provided in any ship of the period. There was accommodation for 120 first class and 20 second class passengers, with provision for berths for another 100 if required. The crew consisted of 60 officers and men.

The vessel was propelled by a pair of side-lever engines of 450 nominal hp, with cylinders 73·5 in diameter by 7 ft stroke. Steam at a pressure of 5 lb per sq in was supplied by four iron return-flue boilers, each with three furnaces. These boilers were, however, replaced in 1844 by tubular boilers. The bunkers provided for 800 tons of coal, but normally not more than 600 tons were carried. The fuel consumption was about 30 tons per day. The paddle-wheels, 28·75 ft diameter, were of the cycloidal form introduced by J. Field in 1833.

The *Great Western* crossed the Atlantic in 1838 in 15 days 5 hours at a mean speed of 8·8 knots. She continued on the Atlantic run until 1846, making 64 crossings in all. In 1847 she was sold to the Royal Mail Steam Packet Co and for 10 years ran between Southampton and the West Indies. She was broken up in 1857.

10 P.S. 'Britannia', 1840

The paddle-steamer *Britannia* was the first vessel built for the British and North American Royal Mail Steam Packet Co, which later became known as the Cunard Steamship Co Ltd. She was constructed of wood by Robert Duncan and Co at Greenock and launched on the 5th February 1840. Her three sister-ships, the *Acadia*, the *Caledonia* and the *Columbia*, were also built on the Clyde about the same time. These four vessels were built to establish a monthly transatlantic mail steamship service from Liverpool to Halifax and Boston, subsidised by the British Government. The *Britannia* was the first steamer built to carry the mails between Great Britain and America.

Rigged as a three-masted barque, the *Britannia* was 228 ft long. The passenger accommodation consisted of the dining saloon and cabins for 115 on the main deck. The vessel was propelled by a pair of side-lever engines contructed by Robert Napier, having cylinders 72 in with a stroke of 6 ft 10 in, and of 440 nominal hp. Steam at a pressure of 9 lb per sq in was supplied by four return-flue boilers each with three furnaces. The paddle-wheels, each with 21 fixed radial floats, had a diameter of 28 ft and the normal speed of the vessel was about 8·5 knots.

The *Britannia* left Liverpool for her first crossing of the Atlantic on the 4th July 1840. She arrived at Halifax in 11 days 4 hours, at a mean speed of 10 knots, and completed her run to Boston in 14 days 8 hours. The return crossing was made in a little over 10 days; the best steaming was 280 miles in one day.

The *Britannia* completed 40 crossings of the Atlantic and in 1849 she was sold to the German Government.

11 S.S. 'Great Britain', 1843

The *Great Britain*, the first screw-propelled iron vessel to cross the Atlantic, was built at Bristol in 1839-43, to the plans of I. K. Brunel, for the Great Western Steamship Co. The hull, 322 ft long, was divided into six water-tight compartments. Accommodation was provided for about 360 passengers.

The original engines of 1000 nominal hp had four inclined cylinders each having a diameter of 88 in with a 6 ft stroke, working upwards on to the crankshaft from which the motion was taken down to the propeller shaft by four sets of flat pitch chains. A six-bladed propeller was fitted and on trials the vessel attained a speed of 11 knots.

The *Great Britain* left Liverpool for New York on the 26th July 1845, with 60 passengers and over 600 tons of cargo, the crossing took 14 days 21 hours at a mean speed of 9·3 knots.

Her transatlantic service ended in 1846 when she went ashore on the coast of Ireland. She remained on the beach all the winter, but was refloated and taken back to Liverpool. After repairs, the vessel was refitted with geared engines having two oscillating cylinders, and a three-bladed propeller.

The *Great Britain* entered the Australian trade in 1852, on which she remained for more than twenty years. Her engines were removed in 1882 and she was converted into a sailing vessel. Since 1886 the *Great Britain* has been a hulk at Port Stanley, in the Falkland Islands.

12 P.S. 'Empire', 1843

Speed and comfortable accommodation for a large number of passengers were of first importance for the passenger boats used on some of the waterways of the United States of America.

The *Empire* built of wood in 1843 for service on the river Hudson between New York and Troy, is a typical example of the fast American river-boat of the mid 19th century.

The hull, with fine lines, was 307 ft long with a beam of only 30·5 ft, but the breadth over the paddle-wheels was 62·5 ft. Longitudinal strength was provided by strong trusses supported by vertical posts. The guards or overhanging sponson decks were supported by the projecting main deck beams. Passengers were accommodated in two tiers of cabins and saloons on the upper and guard decks.

The engines, of the half-beam type, had two immense cylinders having a diameter of 48 in and a stroke of 12 ft, while the paddle-wheels were 32 ft in diameter.

After being sunk in a collision in 1849, the *Empire* was raised and returned to service, but after a further collision in 1853 she was dismantled.

EMPIRE
EMPIRE.

13 Danube Passenger Steamer, 1846

The suitability of steamers for transport on rivers was soon realised and by 1820 steamers had appeared on rivers in America, France, Germany, Great Britain and Russia.

Steam-boats were first used on the Danube in 1830 and this model represents a paddle steamer built of wood at Budapest and launched in September 1846.

The hull followed the usual fine lines for fast river steamers of the period. The steamer was 237 ft long with a beam of 19·5 ft while the breadth over the paddle wheels was 37 ft. The sponsons fitted fore and aft of her paddle-wheels extended further than in contemporary British practice, but not so far as with the American river steamers.

The paddle wheels had a diameter of 20 ft and the speed of the vessel would have been about 12 knots.

14 P.S.S. 'Great Eastern', 1858

This huge steamship, 692 ft long on the upper deck and of 18,914 gross tonnage, was built of iron by J. Scott Russell and Co at Millwall in 1853-8. For thirty years she remained the longest vessel afloat and it was not until 1899 that her dimensions were exceeded. The hull-form of the *Great Eastern* followed the lines that had for many years been adopted by J. Scott Russell, embodying his 'wave-line' principle. I. K. Brunel, however, proposed the use of the two systems of propulsion (see overleaf) and also the cellular construction of the hull. From the keel to the water-line, the hull was double, while the deck was also cellular, which contributed to the longitudinal strength of the hull. Accommodation was provided for 4,000 passengers. She had five funnels and six masts, which could spread 6,500 sq yds of canvas.

The *Great Eastern's* first voyage across the Atlantic was made in June 1860; the greatest speed attained during the passage was 14·5 knots, the average speed being 14 knots. Owing, however, to her relatively small engine-power and low speed the ship was never a commercial success either as a passenger or a cargo steamer, and her most valuable work was done between 1865 and 1873 when she was engaged in laying a number of submarine cables, an employment for which her great size made her especially suitable. After this she did no useful work and was sold in 1888 as scrap metal and eventually broken up.

15 P.S.S. 'Great Eastern', amidships

The *Great Eastern* was unique in that she was propelled both by paddle-wheels and by a screw propeller.

The paddle engines, of the oscillating type, were designed and constructed by John Scott Russell and Co. The cylinders, four in number, had a diameter of 74 in and a stroke of 14 ft. Two of the cylinders drove one crank, and the other two a crank at right-angles, on a built-up paddle shaft. There were two air pumps driven by a single crank on the intermediate length of the paddle shaft, and there were two independent condensers and reversing gears so that each paddle-wheel, driven by a complete double cylinder engine, could be run alone if required. The engines, of 1,000 nominal hp, and 3,411 indicated hp, weighed 836 tons. Steam at 24 lb per sq in pressure was supplied by four double-ended tubular boilers. The original paddle-wheels had a diameter of 56 ft and weighed 90 tons each.

The screw engines, of 1,600 nominal hp were constructed by James Watt and Co, and had four horizontal direct-acting cylinders, each having a diameter of 84 in and a stroke of 4 ft, giving a total indicated 4,890 hp. Steam was supplied by a further six tubular boilers. The four-bladed, cast-iron propeller had a diameter of 24 ft.

16 P.S. 'Connaught', 1860

This paddle-steamer and three sister ships, the *Ulster, Munster* and *Leinster* were built for the mail service between Holyhead and Kingston. They together marked a considerable advance in fast packet construction and proved very reliable in service. In the interests of speed, full advantage was taken of iron hull construction to build them long and narrow with extra strength, so as to provide ample resistance to the severe shocks which these vessels encountered when driven at full speed in a rough sea.

The hull of the *Connaught* was 338 ft long and subdivided by nine water-tight bulkheads. The engines had two oscillating cylinders, each with a diameter of 98 in and a stroke of 6 ft 6 in, which developed about 2,750 indicated hp. Steam at 20 lb per sq in pressure was supplied by eight tubular boilers, four placed forward and four aft of the engine. The speed of the vessel was about 18·2 knots.

The *Connaught* remained in service until 1897, when she was sold to French shipowners, and was broken up in 1898.

17 P.S. 'Scotia', 1861

The twenty years since the *Britannia* (Plate 10) was launched had seen great improvements in shipbuilding. Iron construction had brought greater size, water-tight bulkheads and greater resistance to vibration, and screw propulsion had become firmly established. After 1865, all large ocean-going vessels were screw-propelled.

The *Scotia* was the last and finest of the paddle-steamers to be built for the Cunard Steamship Co's transatlantic service. She was built of iron at Glasgow and at the time of her launch in 1861 she was said to be the strongest-built merchant steamer afloat; her gross register was 3,871 tons and her length 400 ft; there was accommodation for 300 passengers and 1,400 tons of cargo could be carried.

Her paddle-wheels, 40 ft in diameter, were driven by a pair of side-lever engines of 975 nominal hp. These had cylinders having a diameter of 100 in and a stroke of 12 ft, which indicated 4,570 hp. Steam at 25 lb per sq in pressure was supplied by eight tubular boilers.

The fastest Atlantic crossing of the *Scotia* was 8 days 3 hours; she held the Blue Riband from 1862 to 1867 and remained on the North Atlantic service for 13 years. In 1879 the *Scotia* was converted into a twin-screw ship and fitted with compound-expansion engines. Her water-tight bulkheads saved her when a severe explosion blew out her bows some years later and she survived until wrecked in 1904.

18 P.S. 'Colonel Lamb', 1864

During the American Civil War, as the Northern blockade grew more effective, special ships were built as blockade runners and the *Colonel Lamb* is stated to have been the largest and most successful of those built for the Confederacy in Great Britain. High speed and a low silhouette were necessary, and also shallow draught, to be relatively independent of tides in coastal waters. Since, in addition, sufficient strength to face a possible hurricane was required, the builders used steel, then so new a material for shipbuilding that this is believed to be the first steel hull ever to cross an ocean.

The *Colonel Lamb*, built at Liverpool, was 296 ft long, schooner-rigged, and fitted with oscillating engines of 350 nominal hp. Steam was supplied by two sets of boilers, one forward and one aft of the engine-room and the vessel was capable of a speed of about 17 knots.

She proved very troublesome to the Northerners and fear of her seems to have been most pronounced. A report from the US Consulate in Liverpool in 1864 states. 'I regard her as a very superior steamer. If armed with one or two guns she would be able to do much mischief as a privateer.' Her adventurous career ended violently. At the end of the Civil War, having been sold to the Brazilian Government, she was chartered to take a cargo of explosives across the Atlantic, but blew up while at anchor in the Mersey.

19 S.S. 'City of Paris', 1865

The Atlantic liner *City of Paris*, the first of that name, was built of iron at Glasgow and launched in December 1865 for the service of the Liverpool, New York and Philadelphia Steamship Co (Inman Line) between Liverpool and New York. The Inman Line was founded in 1850, but not until 1866 did it make a bid for speed supremacy on the Atlantic, with this vessel which held the Blue Riband from 1867 to 1872.

The hull, 358ft long, was constructed with bulkheads which afforded a water-tight subdivision far in advance of contemporary practice.

The vessel was at first propelled by horizontal simple expansion direct-acting trunk engines of 500 nominal hp, with two cylinders each having a diameter of 82in and a stroke of 3ft 6in, which developed a total of 2,600 indicated hp. Steam at a pressure of 30lb per sq in was supplied by 8 rectangular fire-tube boilers heated by 24 furnaces which consumed 105 tons of coal per day. In 1870 the vessel was lengthened to 397ft and thereby increased from 2,651 tons gross register to 3,081 tons. In 1881 she was refitted with two-stage expansion engines of 550 nominal hp, with cylinders having a diameter of 44·5in and 84in, both with a stroke of 5ft, and supplied with steam at a pressure of 80lb per sq in. The screw propeller was three-bladed and the service speed of the vessel was about 12·5 knots.

Her record Atlantic crossing was made in 1867, from Queenstown to New York in 8 days 4 hours 1 minute at a mean speed of 13·77 knots.

In 1879, the *City of Paris* served as a transport for the Zulu war, and was stranded on a rock in Simon's Bay. She was refloated, however, and finally lost at sea in March 1885 as the result of a collision.

20 P.S. 'Inez Clarke', 1879

In the more remote parts of the world speed was not always of major importance and the hulls of tropical river steamers were often little more than rectangular pontoons with the forward corners rounded.

The *Inez Clarke* was one of a pair of steel stern-wheel paddle-steamers built in London for the Government of Colombia, for the mail service on the Magdalena River.

Very shallow draught and resistance to floating timber were required – hence the triple rudders and stern-wheel instead of side paddles, and the deep trusses with screw adjustment which were introduced to avoid vibration and provide longitudinal strength. These also formed the supports for the two upper decks, upon which the saloon accommodation was provided. The hull, 130 ft long, was divided into eight water-tight compartments. These vessels could attain a speed of over 13 knots.

The 'locomotive' boiler, with a large grate suitable for burning wood, was placed forward in order to distribute the weight. The compound-expansion engines were of 250 indicated hp, but there was an arrangement for obtaining extra power for a short space of time when ascending rapids. The fan which supplied the forced draught to the furnace and ventilation to the saloons was driven by an engine which also drove a circular saw for cutting up the wood fuel.

Science Museum illustrated booklets

Other titles in this series:

Timekeepers Clocks, watches, sundials, sand-glasses

Ship Models Part 1: From earliest times to 1700 AD

Ship Models Part 2: Sailing ships from 1700 AD

Ship Models Part 3: British Small Craft

Ship Models Part 4: Foreign Small Craft

Railways Part 1: To the end of the 19th century

Chemistry Part 1: Chemical Laboratories and Apparatus to 1850

Chemistry Part 2: Chemical Laboratories and Apparatus from 1850

Chemistry Part 3: Atoms, Elements and Molecules

Chemistry Part 4: Making Chemicals

Aeronautics Part 1: Early Flying up to the Reims meeting

Aeronautics Part 2: Flying since 1913

Power to Fly Aircraft Propulsion

Aeronautica Objets d'Art, Prints, Air Mail

Lighting Part 1: Early oil lamps, candles

Lighting Part 2: Gas, mineral oil, electricity

Making Fire Wood friction, tinder boxes, matches

Cameras Photographs and Accessories

Agriculture Hand tools to Mechanization

Fire Engines and other fire-fighting appliances

Astronomy Globes, Orreries and other Models

Surveying Instruments and Methods

Physics for Princes The George III Collection

Motor Cars up to 1930

Published by
Her Majesty's Stationery Office
and obtainable from the
Government Bookshops listed
on cover page iv (post orders
to PO Box 569 London SE1)

7s each (by post 7s 4d)

Printed in England for
Her Majesty's Stationery Office
by W. Heffer & Sons Ltd.
Cambridge

Dd. 142400 K100